Out Of Darkness

Into Light

Poetry by
Lin Brian

Copyright © 2017 Lin Brian

All rights reserved.

ISBN-13:978-1542585286

ISBN-10:1542585287

Lake Havasu City, AZ
www.EasytimePublishing.com

CONTENTS

Acknowledgments	vi
Forward	viii
Prayer	1
Abusers	2
The Roar	3
Let Me Die Now	4
Sleep	5
We, The Children	6
Splitting	9
Grateful	10
Victim No More	13
Survival	14
Who Am I?	15
The Scream	16
As A Leaf Grows	17
Freeze-Frame	18
Terror	20
Need	21
Parts of Me	22
Dying	23
If You Could Just See...	24
Death	26
Understand	27
Good Friends	28
Two Touches	29
Pain	30
Dare to Dream	31
The Gift	32
Fear	33
Gone	34
Why Do You Weep?	35
He	36
Red Blood	38
Standing	40
Fractured	42
Drugs	43
Where I Want To Be	44
Despair	45
Missing Woman	46

Contents Continued

Therapy	48
Not Guilty	49
The Void	50
Just Be	51
Child	52
My Life	54
Silence	55
Sitting Tall	56
Lost Time	58
Hello Out There!	59
Hurt	60
Blessed Am I	62
Gratitude	63
The Search	64
Getting Better	66
Memories	68
Being a Woman	70
Choose	73
Whip	74
The Family Waiting	76
Blame	77
Leaf	78
Hey Mom	79
Suicide	80
What A Ride	81
Life	82
Not My Business	84
Facets Program	86
Hatred	87
Games	88
Rage	89
The Vagina Monologues	90
Evil	92
Lonely	94
Friends	95
My Friend	96
Support	97
Insight	98
Time	100
Talking	101
Gotta Leave	102

Contents Continued

Free	104
Choices	105
Beauty	106
Help	107
Abuse	108
Change	109
Choose You	110
Freeing Me	112
Smile	113
About the Author	114

ACKNOWLEDGMENTS

A myriad of people have helped make this book possible. My husband, Edward Filiatrault, has supported and loved me, even when I wasn't lovable and has taken up the slack when my mind was on writing. My late Mother, Pearl Tammie, told me I could do anything. She believed in me implicitly. My daughter, Daina Brian, and my son, Ritchie Brian, have read and put their seal of approval on many of my earlier poems. I owe a debt of gratitude to my life-long friend, Pat Armishaw, for helping me find my way when I felt lost. My sister-in-law, Pat Lane gently pushed me forward...sometimes not so gently, telling me I **have to** get this book out there. To my girlfriends who have been the recipient of many of my poems over the years, a heartfelt thank you for listening, encouraging and believing. Thank-you, B.J. Alexander, for helping to keep me grounded. Our weekday walks and sharing mean the world to me. Louise Lapierre, our laughter makes life a joy. Noreen Dorais, your loving support is invaluable. Linda Cipolla, you honoured me by sharing some of my poetry with your group. Our souls are connected. Ursula Wick, your wisdom, genius, critiquing and graphics have inspired. And thanks to the countless others who have encouraged along life's way. Of the many therapists through the years, Roxie Van Aller and Sheila Robertson have been instrumental in helping me learn to free myself. Thank you.

This book would not have come to fruition yet had I not met Paul Bailey, of Easytime Publishing last year. It has been a joy working with him. He has made this labour of love come alive. Paul, thank you. Your company name speaks for itself.

Look for Paul L. Bailey's book "The Rich Boys" later this year, featuring two poems by Lin.

Forward

These poems are not for the faint-of-heart.

They chronicle one woman's thoughts and feelings as she worked her way 'Out of Darkness Into Light'.

They are for those remembering horrific abuses perpetrated against them. They are for the survivors stuck in a place of remembering, of actually re-living the horror and fearing they won't ever get out. While the story may be different, the feelings that wash over us like tidal waves are the same. We hurt. We despair. The pain is so great we want to die. We feel life isn't worth living. We know at a core level we have no worth, that we deserve whatever happens to us. We set ourselves up for more abuse and the cycle continues.

The good news is the cycle can be broken! There can be joy after abuse.

These poems are meant to give hope to those without hope of a better life.

What happened to you was ***not*** your fault. You deserve to have joy in your life.

Prayer

Heal my body...
Heal my soul...
Heal my spirit...
Make me whole.

ABUSERS

It is written. It is true.
An abuser wants all of you.
Not content with only heart,
they need all of us. It isn't smart
to put a cage around a soul,
in every way attempt control
what we should think, what we should do.
After all, we're human, too!
And we will learn to break away,
and you can never make us stay.
I want my life. It's mine, you see,
and you can't have it, it's for me.
At last, to live the life I choose,
while in your hate, you lose. You lose.

THE ROAR

The things they did,
the lies they told,
to get possession of my soul.
I cannot speak of things I've done.
The memories shame and I must run
into a place that safe for me.
I block again the memory.

For years my past was buried deep
enough inside, as if asleep.
But now the sleeping lions roar,
demand a voice, are still no more.
And I no longer can resist.
And I'm petrified. But they insist.

LET ME DIE NOW

Healing tears. Forgetful sleep.
How did I get in so deep?
I can't remember how to cope.
Everything gone. I've lost my hope.
Friends. Friends. Friends I held so dear
are gone. They do not wish to hear.
All alone. There's only me.
I can't get out. I've lost the key.
I can't get out. It hurts my head.
That's who I am. The walking dead.
Caught half in this world. Half in that.
The light's gone out, and all is black.
Don't like this life where I try, try, try.
I want to go now. I want to die.

SLEEP

Merciful sleep pulls me down again.
I surrender to the drug that numbs me.
It helped me survive years of abuse.
I was beginning to know something was wrong
and I would have to make some painful decisions.
I could leave or die.
The death of my soul was certain had I stayed.

As I sort my life, I grow.
I learn about self-esteem and find ways to develop mine.
I learn other ways of coping.
I learn tools that help me through the worst.
I learn more about others
and am able to better express caring.
Life gets better and better and better.
When I get to a rough spot,
sleep helps me through.

WE, THE CHILDREN

For all of those who do not know
I will use my voice,
to speak for all the children
who do not have a choice.
For those who do not make it,
let us say a prayer.
Let's shout it from the rooftops.
There are those of us who care.

Imagine being three years old
with no one you can tell
that your father is molesting you,
that you live your days in hell.
Even worse is speaking
when no one will believe
a child of three against a man
with the talent to deceive.

Our mother cannot stop it...
even though she knows.
She does not protect us
from all those vicious blows.
Being told it's our fault
is something we believe.
It steals the very soul from us.
For our lost life we grieve.

My brother tries protecting me,
but he is only eight
and cannot stop our father
from venting all his hate.
Using leather belt and fists
to hurt and bruise and maim,
while we, the little children
will never be the same.

Because we cannot stand the pain
our mind divides in two.
We pretend it is not happening.
We pretend it isn't true.
Our life blood slowly seeping out.
There's nothing left inside.
Our life a ball of misery
as we try to run and hide.

Eventually we stop trying
and simply want to die.
We are extremely tired
when all we do is try
to be good in every way
so our father will not touch
in any way at all that hurts.
We're not asking much.

And here's the biggest payoff.
It is the very worst.
We think that we deserve it
when all we've been is cursed.
We've been abused as children.
Please listen to our plea!
STOP the monsters hurting us
and bring some help to me!

SPLITTING

How many ways can I split?
How many times will I try?
Right now I'm feeling like shit.
Right now I wish I could die.

GRATEFUL

Grateful for our time together...
Grateful that we shared...
Grateful for your knowledge...
Grateful that you cared.

The work we did has changed me.
Now *know* I have a choice.
With each and every meeting
I learned to use my voice.

That very voice was choked from me
by abuse when I was young.
Taught me I had no value,
and living with that stung.

We find ways to make a life
that 'chooses' more abuse.
One day life's not worth living
and we figure it's no use.

We cannot escape the very hell
of knowing we are bad.
That we deserve what comes our way
and Oh My God – that's sad.

And then the outside world shines in
and we begin to see
that others can live differently.
I wanted that for me!

The black cloud of my doubt dissolved.
I knew I had to find
someone to walk me from my shame,
to help me clear my mind.

A mind so very muddled
that it could just not see
that it was my abuser's fault.
The fault was not with me.

And so the longest search began
to find the help I need.
Of course it has been worth it
and I no longer bleed.

But oh, it's taken lifetimes
more than twenty years.
Each person gave me what they could
but nothing stopped the tears.

Then about four years ago
our paths, well, they connected.
We mapped a different way for me.
Understanding was injected.

The work has not been easy.
So glad to find the way
to make a lasting difference.
There dawns a brand new day.

And I don't think that you can know
the gratitude I feel
for you, your help, and knowledge
Today I am more real...

No longer hide myself away
from others, lest they find
I am no good as I've been told.
Today, I have my mind!

And now it's time for you to go...
I know we've had our season.
I trust the Universe is right.
for all, there is a reason.

VICTIM NO MORE

At last, she shed her cloak of victimhood,
squared her shoulders strong and stood
up straight as though a winner proud,
nodded her head, and asked out loud.

"Oh My. Oh My. Can this really be?
I've found myself. And I feel free.
No longer chained by those who prey
on weakened folk. I've found my way.
There will be times that I will fail,
and hurt, and cry, and sometimes wail.
But I am victim never more.
This is what I'm living for!"

SURVIVAL

Sometimes we feel beaten
and hurt right to the core.
Bruised inside and life's too hard.
We can't take it anymore.

All we can do is survive each day...
we swear that we're insane.
Remember... Surviving is what we do
until we live again!!

WHO AM I?

Hardly flattering.
Shattering.
Reversing.
Rehearsing.
My image of myself.

Smoking.
Choking.
Changes.
Rearranges.
Until I am wrung out and confused.

Who am I???

THE SCREAM

The scream sits in my throat.
Silent.
My head pounds. My back aches.
The lid is clamped on so tightly,
sealed by years of forcing it down.
If I could only scream perhaps I would find relief.

AS A LEAF GROWS

As the leaf grows from the bud,
so do I now,
from the part of me
that survived.

New life.
Not knowing what I will become.
Struggling to wholeness
we cling to the branch.

At times our hold is fragile.
At others... secure.

Growing daily,
though the naked eye can't see.
At times I would let go, yet I cling.

There is a thread to life that holds me.

FREEZE-FRAME

Do you think I like a bloody head?
I am caught in a place where I don't know
whether to freeze or thaw.
I am a freeze-frame photo,
snapped in a position of anguish,
catatonic,
trying to swallow pain.
It will not be swallowed and yet,
there is no safe place
for me to vomit.
I force myself into inaction
while my mind
sees my fist go through the mirror,
through the windshield,
my hands beating the car doors,
my arms flailing at the ground
with a stick.

Do you think I like a bloody head?
You say I should give it a rest.
That my pain is too much for me.
You are worried for me.
Are you?
Really?
Or are you worried for yourself?

I can understand.
It is not pleasant to see me.
It is not pleasant to be me, either,
but... I am all I've got.
And I need to spew this pain out,
this pain that has a million sources.
And my head is going to get a lot bloodier
before I quit bleeding.
You had better decide if you can stand
the sight of blood because I cannot promise
that I can only bleed quietly
when you are not at home.

TERROR

Every night the terror returns,
waking me at 3:00 a.m.
Wide awake, my agony burns.
Nameless.
Faceless.
Fear seethes, gripping my spirit so tight
I...
...can't
...breathe.

NEED

Out of my need to be different...
Out of my need to be free...
Out of my need to change what I was,
a new world is waiting for me.
I can't always be what you want me to be.
I just need to be who I am.
Not easy, you know. It takes a long while.
I can do it! Yes, do it I can.
If you can accept the person I am
knowing full well it is choice,
we will both win, yes, both of us will.
That is a cause to rejoice.

PARTS OF ME

Parts of me are missing,
don't know if they'll be found.
Did they simply disappear?
Are they trampled in the ground?
Perhaps if I keep looking
maybe then I'll find
all the missing pieces
that once made up my mind.
For it is darkness of despair
that makes us feel insane.
Look up! See sun! Hang on,
and you'll feel whole again!

DYING

To be understood would be
life's greatest gift to me.
It does not seem that others can bear
to see me in so much pain,
so I should hide it...
only allow the pain,
only do my work
when they are safely away from here
so that they will not have to see
who I am,
what I feel,
and I will pretend to be what they want,
like I have done all of my life.

IF YOU COULD JUST SEE...

If you could just see yourself as others see you...
How often have I thought this about others
who are struggling with the pain of feeling worthless,
without applying it to myself?
Why am I the last one to see my own worth?
Why must I go through others' pain
before I can allow myself to feel mine?

"They" are worthy.
"They" deserve better treatment,
and yet my soul cries out in anguish,
"What about me?"
How long am I destined to be stuck in this place?
A place where pain sits in my throat
begging to be expelled, and yet, I know...
I know I need a safe place to let go
and someone safe to let go with
so that I can come back.
I need someone to help me come back.
It is a measure of the depth of feeling
to have buried it so deeply.
But now it has moved from begging, to insisting.
It will not be kept down.
It is like vomit, moving up and out of its own accord
as I try in vain to keep it in.

Hot tears stain my face and sometimes I move
into the pain and it is ripped out of the centre of
my being in harsh howling as I lay there hyperventilating,
curled up in a ball.
It washes over me like the tides. Again and again and again.
I breathe, as if to give birth, and, in a sense, I am –
giving birth to the pain I have not acknowledged
so that it can come up and out of me.
So that it will hurt a little less.
And life goes on.

DEATH

And so, this is death,
this desire not to feel,
this shutting down of feelings
that I developed in self-defence,
when I had no other tools
and no other choice.
Now I am an adult
and I have a choice.

UNDERSTAND

You want me to quit reading for awhile,
to take a break from my pain.
You do not understand.
There is no such choice for me,
for only in the reading can I validate my life,
my feelings, and I deserve that.

Only in knowing that others have survived
this incredible pain of discovery.
Knowing they, too, have lost part of their lives
to abuse, helps me accept my truth.
If I were alone in this it would be unbearable.

I do not have names for all of the pain I feel.
I need to name them and grieve them.
Then I can let them go.

I am ready.
It sits inside me like poison
and only when I dissociate
do I find a little peace.
But my "off" button is getting weaker
and now sometimes does not work at all.

It is my time.
I need to look at this,
the whole package,
once and for all,
for only in seeing will I be able to live again.

GOOD FRIENDS

Good friends are the fragrance
in my garden, a sunrise to behold.
They are my favourite music,
bring me happiness untold.

I see in them the flowers.
I feel in them the sun.
I hear in them the realness,
and I love them, every one.

TWO TOUCHES

There are two different touches;
the touch that feels like love,
that encourages the bird to wing,
and the touch that feels like possession,
that attempts to chain a soul.

That touch is a killing touch.

Would that I am free,
for I have felt them both...
and it is interesting
that the loving touch
binds me to him still.

PAIN

The pain, the pain. My pain
pierces my soul like icy rain.
It makes my world turn inside out,
saps my strength and makes me doubt
my sanity, my will to live.
Oh God, how much more must I give
to still the horrors of my past
and feel serenity at last.

DARE TO DREAM

I walk on air because,
finally and forever,
I dare to dream.
In so doing, I begin
to envision a positive life for me,
for all things are possible
if I but believe.

Gone the woman who wanted to die.
Gone the feeling of total helplessness,
as an infant is helpless.
Like a baby still, yet different
in that now I see the world
as one big opportunity
waiting for me to explore.

Is it a matter of perception?
What has changed?
My personal work on me has
changed me irrevocably.

And you can do the same.
For I am no more special than you.
We are all unique and special.

Come walk with me.

THE GIFT

Amidst the weeds the flowers grow
straight and true. Their colours show
they have won the battle to survive.
And even more, they live to thrive.

Living, breathing, they impart
peace and love within the heart.
Peace and love, for everything.
Behold the beauty that they bring.

All shapes. All sizes. Ah… the smell.
Their therapy can make you well.
Partake. Drink up the joy. It's free.
It is a gift from them to me.
You can share it, feel it, too.
It is the gift they give to you.

FEAR

What colour is my fear?
Is it black or grey?
What colour is my fear today?
Is it orange? Is it brown?
What colour is my fear?
Will it always bring me down?
Make me feel I'll surely drown?
What colour is my fear?
Will it always be so near?
Will it ever go away?
Will I ever learn to play?
What colour is my fear today?

GONE

Time stops.
Noises fade.
Into my mind.
Vaguely aware that once again
I have escaped
into a place
where I have spent
too many hours
as a child
to protect myself.

Now...
I am an adult
and
no longer need to hide.
I can cope.
I can heal.
Awareness first, then change.
Why must I still leave like this?

WHY DO YOU WEEP?

"Why do you weep?" they ask.
"Because I was sexually abused as a child," I say.
"But that's over. You're an adult now.
Get on with your life," they say.
"My life was taken by my abuser," I say.
"Forget it. Get on with your life now," they repeat.
"My life?" I question. "I don't even know who I am.
I hid myself so totally so that others would not know,
that I even hid myself from myself."

They look at me uncomprehendingly.

"I kept quiet because I was ashamed, but
now I can see that it was not my fault
and I will not carry my secret any longer," I explain.
"Why are you dredging up all of this now?" they ask.

And I see that I have not reached them,
but the world needs to know,
and I will keep quiet no longer
because of their judgments.

"Why do you weep?" they ask.

HE

I feel as if he chewed me up
and spit me out.
I wonder if he would have
if he'd known that I would sprout.

He doesn't seem to have
self-love enough to know
that the more pieces that I am
gives me more from which to grow.

Although it's been four years plus
he is trying still
to control my life, to wound me,
to bend to his will.
To hurt and maim as in the past
and make my spirit die.
Although I've gotten stronger,
he still can make me cry.

I know I know the answer,
but still I question why
he doesn't get a better life
instead of only getting by
on concrete hate and anger,
saying things not true
for when he hurts me the most,
I know what I must do.

Focus on my own life,
spend time with a friend.
Seek out those who love me...
there seems to be no end
of people who I value
and who seem to value me.
For now I feel cared for,
and live with dignity.

RED BLOOD

Red blood on soft white fur,
darkening, drying, hardening,
making a mockery of what used to be.
Broken rabbits, mangled beyond repair.

Three rabbits.
One for each year of my young life...
Murdered.
To show me what would happen
to me and my family
if I ever told.

And so.
I didn't.
For thirty-nine years, I "forgot".
And for thirty-nine years
I was like the rabbits...
broken,
mangled inside.

The few memories I now have explain so much.
Why I needed to please
at the expense of my own spirit.
Why I am so devastated by anger.
Why I've spent most of my life
in a frozen state.
To feel hurt too much.
Why I've been so afraid all of my life.
Unknown fears.

Can you believe one man's sickness can steal a life?

STANDING

I will not be stepped on like a stone, though I was for years,
nor be controlled by a man who I no longer fear.
I am not a doormat. I won't allow myself to be.
I can see the difference. I am learning to be free.

Though the light took long to come, I'm grateful that it came.
It has so greatly changed me. I'll never be the same.
The more I start to understand, the more I need to know.
The knowledge I am craving will always help me grow.

The need to know yet even more burns within me deep
and by my hand my pencil writes the secrets that I keep.
Who else knows the depths of pain that has been mine alone
for accepting other's rules and making them my own?

No longer must I be the one to give and give and give,
and tend to everybody's needs. I, as well, must live.
My needs are important, too. I can see that now.
To have anyone pretend they're not, I will not allow.

I must seek direction. I know not where to turn.
But the life I seek is mine alone, and for it I yearn.
The answers are not easy. Seeking takes its toll.
For me, there is no other way to satisfy my soul.

The vacuum that I lived in I no longer can accept.
The rules that I was living by no longer can be kept.
Who can tell me how to live and what type I must be?
No! Not ever anyone. My need is to be free.

I must be my own judge, by my own rules live.
No one else has the right to tell me what to give.
And so I seek inside myself and search outside as well,
the answers that I greatly need to take me from this hell.

This hell of being put down because I will not do
or be the serving person that others want me to.
Important. Yes. Important to know that I can give,
but not when, no, not when others tell me how to live.

FRACTURED

Out of it.
But where am I?
Can't focus.
Feel dead.
What's going on?

Go where?
Vaguely aware that
there are others in this room.

Can't stay.
Gotta go.
Go where?
Do what?
Gotta get these feelings out,
but I don't know what they are...

DRUGS

I dress up, go out and stand out in the rain.
There is just no damn way to escape from the pain.
I hate the johns and I hate the tricks,
but tell me how else I'll get my next fix.
No way to get off this roller-coaster ride,
feel a gripping need to run and hide.
Hide from life and live no more,
there's gotta be more on a different shore.
Then when I stick the needle in my arm
I feel powerful and free from all harm.
My insecurities disappear. And I am very strong.
And I now know, without a doubt. Of course, I **do** belong!
The minutes pass. I'm down again. Back in that black hole.
Each time that I fall into it, falling takes its toll.
And yes! They tell me addiction can be kicked.
What's waiting for me if I manage it, is so awfully sick.
I know I'm full of memories, full of night-time terror.
I know my whole damn life has been just one big error.
I'm stuck in this drugged up world, and for that I'm truly sorry.
I know as I sink lower, my loved ones wait and worry.
And I just don't know what to do to change the way I am.
Who cares, anyway? I know *I* don't give a damn!!!

WHERE I WANT TO BE

Where healing women gather,
that's where I want to be.
Where sharing, love and caring
are given willingly.
Where words are spoken
that empower the soul,
where we struggle together
to make ourselves whole,
where arms reach out
to support and to hold,
and the warmth of togetherness
keeps us from cold.
Where we try to be honest,
address what we feel,
while daily, each of us,
becoming more real.
I have definitely decided
that this is for me...
Where healing women gather,
that's where I want to be.

DESPAIR

In the depths of despair I walk alone.
Lonely and desolate, I shut myself away
from those who don't feel safe.
I submerge into blackness, alone and afraid,
unable to reach out to connect.
My soul is dry. There is nothing but pain in my world.
Darkness overtakes and I cave in upon myself
until the only thing left in this seething mass of misery
is the tiny flicker that knows I have to wait
until this passes.
This is survival.

MISSING WOMEN

Alas she had no family, 'cept ladies of the street.
There was no one else in this whole world
to care when she'd be beat.
No one else who gave a shit whether she lived or died.
More than once she gave up. And more than once she cried,
wondering again just what she did to live a life like this,
wondering if God forgot her. She no longer felt His kiss,
the one that gently touched her cheek
and told her she was good.
Why has He gone? Where is He? She wished she understood.

You know we won't forget you... the butterflies in your hair.
What a harsh way you chose to get from here to there.
We didn't know where you had gone...
and we didn't know why.
But over time, we figured it out, pieced it together by and by.
And when we knew, we couldn't believe,
and each of us detested
that when you were very young, and no one helped,
you were molested.
Cannot go there often, the memories bring us pain.
so I'll just remember happy times until we meet again.

Always the clown in the family, so quick, so full of wit.
Who'd ever think that you'd get caught up in that shit?
When our home life was bad you'd break the tension
with a joke or a mime too numerous to mention.
And you always made us laugh. You always made us giggle
by what you said, what you did, your hilarious wiggle.
You will always be precious. You will always be my sis.
You will always be loved and you will always be missed.

We will remember you darlin', how you loved
to smell the flowers.
As a little girl you played in the sun for hours
and hours and hours.
Content to play with dollies, content to pet the cat.
Content to dress up in cast off clothes, to try on Mommy's hat.
You'd parade around in clothes too big.
It always made us smile.
And now you're gone forever. But we'll meet up in a while.
We'll meet when our time here is done
and we have gone away.
We'll find you up in heaven. We know you'll show the way.

THERAPY

I'm going to try to write a poem to help you understand
just what it's like to need this help...
when someone lends a hand.
Oh God! We need to learn the tools. We need to learn to speak.
We need to find some sort of peace. Yes! This is what we seek.

To live in such anxiety each day in and out.
To feel that we're unworthy, our minds so full of doubt.
Some have coped with busyness. Some give and give and give,
until worn out and overwhelmed we just don't want to live.

Those who are the lucky ones connect with Desert Sun.
And as we start to learn to trust we know this is the one.
This is the place where we can heal and find new ways of being.
We're given tools. We're listened to, all of which is freeing.

I am learning **not** to run when I get really scared.
I'm finding tools with which to cope with things I never dared.
I can say for certain, after years and years of strife.
Finally. The changes. I have a better life.
With learning and support has evolved a happy me,
who's gotta say, without the help, I wonder where I'd be.

NOT GUILTY

Not guilty, your honour, are the words that he said
as many that gathered wished he were dead.
If inmates could reach him and stick in a knife
then I would be free to resume my old life.
Consumed by rage and hatred, present all these years,
time lost, energy drained, physical pain, infinite tears,
I know I can't move forward until I let go of past.
And I so need to find me again. I do let go at last.
Who gets to say how long we must grieve,
when we won't be full of sorrow?
It will last as long as it lasts and we can't think of tomorrow
until there is a shift inside that lets us know it's time
and I take back my life from the monster.
He can't have it. He can't. It's mine!!!

THE VOID

I'm sitting on the precipice.
I'm sitting on the edge.
And there's just a small fraction
of something I can't name
stopping me from jumping into the void.

JUST BE

I don't want to think. I just want to be.
I just want to know this person called me.
Stop that hamster wheel from spinning ever faster,
time to just sit quietly, let go of that old master.
The one that kept me busy until I would collapse.
The one that always helped me keep my feelings under wraps.
At first it caused anxiety to try to be so still.
My mind and body out of sorts, they tried to run until
I filled the quietness with work and things to fill my mind.
Yet as I practiced stillness, wonders do I find.
I am loving stillness, allowing to reflect
and I accept the part of me I wanted to reject
and in that great acceptance and owning who I am,
I live a life of choosing rather than a sham.
While I did the best I could with my knowledge then,
it brings me joy to get to know who I am again!

CHILD

I may look just like an adult to you,
but I'm still a little child inside.
And when I'm hurting desperately
and can't cope, I run and hide.
Don't minimize my feelings.
Don't deny all of my pain.
For when you do, I'm hurt by you,
and neither of us will gain.
Instead, please honour each feeling.
Remember, I do my best.
The past often leaves me reeling
as I bravely face each test.
I need to express my grieving,
and I need to let it go.
And though I often think of leaving,
I do want to live, I know.
Sometimes, for me, the work is too much.
It overwhelms and brings me down.
And that's when I'm open and am way past hopin'
and feel I'll surely drown.

You can help by being there
and letting me know I'm heard.
That always, somewhere, there are people who care.
That helps me feel assured.
I've learned to accept that it will pass
and my life resume once more.
And I believe one day I will not have to pay
by re-living my childhood horror.

MY LIFE

When I have but one life to give,
then I will decide how *I* want to live.
I need to live in a way that feels true.
Which may be quite different for you.

I recognize that I have a choice,
and continually attempt to use my own voice.
When I end up feeling unheard,
I get to the place where I say... not a word.

I share who I am with those who can hear,
for those are the ones in my heart I hold dear.
I express how I feel, and am not made wrong;
though they might disagree, it's okay. I feel strong.

We all have our feelings. Of this I am sure,
and sharing together is a way to endure
the heartaches in life that we have to bear.
They are lightened when shared with someone to care.

You need to walk your walk. I need to walk mine.
The walks aren't the same. For me, it is time
to soar with the eagles, to try my own wings,
eagerly embracing what living life brings.

SILENCE

My friend, my valued friend,
she hears my lonely cry.
She reads between the painful lines
as I mournfully ask why.

She does *not* attempt to fix me
or mend my broken heart.
She simply listens gracefully
to me. It is the start;
the start of my becoming
a more authentic me.
For in her open silence
she encourages me to be.

SITTING TALL

Once I thought I wasn't there,
until I looked under the chair.
And there I saw a little bear,
curled up tight upon its side,
curled up tight as if to hide
itself away from life's sweet ride.

And on its little face, a frown
that said everything is upside down
and everything is turned around.
If they don't know, and cannot see
then they cannot torture me.
Please. Oh, please. Just let me be.

And no one knew that I was there,
a curled-up bear, under the chair.
And I was glad. I didn't care.
And then one day the other bears
were curled up tight, and under chairs
all hiding from their own nightmares.

I told my tale to other bears
all hiding there, under chairs.
Together, we all shared our cares.
And after time, I got quite strong
and grew to know that they were wrong
and, that, indeed, I do belong.

And so, one day I moved about,
uncurled myself, and I crawled out.
Because, you see, I'd lost all doubt.
And now I like it way up there,
sitting tall upon my chair.
And there I'll stay, this little bear
up on my chair, with other bears.

LOST TIME

As I lay inert
at another day's end,
time lost
as my mind strives to remember
what my body won't forget.

Foggy life disappears
again and again and again
and I see the sun's life
against the trees fade into blackness.

Sweet sadness in knowing
I am setting myself free
as my life
slips through my fingers.

HELLO, OUT THERE! DOES ANYONE HEAR?

My soul cries out
in dark despair.
Does anyone hear me?
Does anyone care?

HURT

Without any care of the damage to me,
a defenceless child who just wanted to be
loved and valued for herself alone.
God I hate them for what they have done!

The message to me that I didn't matter
was what caused my feelings and self-worth to scatter,
to freeze, to numb out, to all go away...
I learned to become a robot by day.
By night I would sleep the sleep of the dead
while terror and horror marched through my head,
'oft unremembered.
When remembered, denied.
Oh God, this explains all the tears I have cried,
why I chose violence, abuse after abuse
that I could not identify. Oh, what's the use?

So I numb out some more, become more a robot.
It's hard to describe, this now life-long habit
of only doing and feeling what others permit
while inside, without knowing, always feeling like shit.
It took me twenty-two years to get out with my life
and to see that I could not still be his wife.

But the fear, oh the fear I have felt is unreal.
This is one of the problems with starting to feel.
We can't have good feelings and not feel the bad,
which is why we shut down all our feelings. How sad.

How chaotic our lives are when we first start to feel.
Sometimes we don't know what's real or unreal.
It overwhelms our senses. We fear we are crazy.
We're depressed. We can't work. We're told we are lazy.

I thank God daily other women have felt
and experienced the things that I have. It's a help
to know I am no longer completely alone.
There's many like me. I see how they have grown.
I see courage, support, and a whole lot of love.
We seem to fit well, like a hand in a glove.
Working together, we will find our way
towards healing. I believe there will come a day
when we've worked through our past
and will function quite well
and no longer still stay so trapped by the hell
of others' actions, for we now use our voice
and don't take abuse. We know there's a choice.

BLESSED AM I

Blessed am I
for I can cry.

And God blessed me
for I can see.

And I can mirror
the things I hear.

I can run
and feel the sun.

I can talk
and I can walk.

I've learned to share
because I care.

I see your soul.
It makes me whole.

And because I feel…
I can heal.

GRATITUDE

I'm grateful for the van I drive.
I'm grateful just to be alive.
I'm grateful for the clothes I wear.
I'm grateful for the friends that care.
I'm grateful I can have a shower,
and grow more grateful by the hour.
The wind, the air, the sweet l'il breeze
that snakes its way through waving trees.
I'm grateful that my eyes can see
and grateful for all that's given me.
My life, my health, my life of leisure.
Reading, writing is my pleasure.
Spending time with valued friends.
It seems 'I'm grateful' never ends.
I'm grateful for the love I feel,
and that I found a way to heal.
Every day there's something new
for which I'm very grateful, too.
The gratitude goes on and on
for my daughters and my son.
So very grateful I can see
how much my mate does value me.
Daily gratitude untold
as I watch my very life unfold.

THE SEARCH

The struggle to have come so far
and have so far to go.
The inner search for a better me
will forever flow.

Once embarked upon, this search
must be carried on.
I was chained into a life;
I was almost gone.

Chained by guilt and chained by what
I was taught to be.
I reached the darkness of despair
'ere I could finally see.

The sickness, the resentment,
the angry thoughts untold;
until I no longer cared...
I didn't have a hold.

I let loose my grip on life,
was living in a trance.
The world was dark. I was lost.
I didn't stand a chance.

Sleep was the drug that helped me through.
I slept both day and night.
When I slept, I didn't think...
Still, something wasn't right.

And blessed sleep did help me through.
It helped me numb the strife.
But I knew I had to make a change
to reclaim my life.

As I seek to find my way,
pray for me. Please pray for me.
I need the strength. I need the help
to make my blind eyes see.

GETTING BETTER

There is something wrong with me,
can't get my shit together.
There is something really wrong.
I hope I soon get better.

Have no desire to sweep or cook
or even visit friends.
Just seem to lay and stare at walls
and hope this feeling ends.

There's nothing that I want to do.
I lay and wonder why
momentum's gone. Don't want to live,
don't even want to cry.

A big black cloud has covered me.
I'm caught inside its net.
Don't even fight it any more,
more tangled I will get.

I grieve the life I thought I had.
I grieve the loss of dreams.
But better that, than stuck in this
where nothing is as seems.

And so I move through days and nights
and though I don't know when,
I know one day the cloud will lift
and I'll want to live again.

There is something wrong with me,
can't get my shit together.
There is something really wrong.
I hope I soon get better.

MEMORIES

Softly stealing through my mind
these memories of old,
catching me so unawares
bring pleasure/pain untold.
the pain of being little,
molested by a man,
the pleasure of reaching out
to touch my newborn's hand.

The pain of broken marriage,
the fear I'd lose my life.
My husband said he'd kill me
if I would not be his wife.
The pleasure as I learned somehow
to be a better me,
to find and use a stronger voice,
to open eyes to see.

The pain of finding love again
and seeing it destroyed.
The pain of feeling nothing's left,
no way to fill the void.
The pleasure that, as time went by
my life evolved again.
I found in my exploring
more than one true friend.

The pain of seeing mother pass,
no longer in my life.
that pain, it sluices through my heart
like sharply honed steel knife.
The pleasure as I find new things
to occupy my time,
and wonderment in knowing
I haven't lost my mind.

Pleasure and much gratitude
in having legs to walk,
ears to hear and eyes to see,
the ability to talk.
Pleasure in the sharing of
the present and the past.
And such pleasure in the knowing
I've found peace at last.

BEING A WOMAN

It took a very long time to get to be me,
an extremely long time for my blind eyes to see,
inordinate time to see the whole truth,
that although I am female, I surely have worth.
Not different from brothers right from the start,
loved by mommy and daddy with all of their heart.
But they could not see the damage to me,
a simple young child who just wanted to be,
who was molested and tortured by an uncle, a man
who screwed with my mind as only he can.
Yes, it's true. There were many years of abuse.
I thought I deserved it. Oh hell! what's the use?
How to determine the good from the bad
took more than the knowledge and courage I had.
'til left at death's door not more than a shell.
Can anyone see me? Can anyone tell?
I grew up. Got married, had children, too.
Of course that is what I expected to do.
Unknowingly picked for myself an abuser,
another sick man, a new 'woman user'.
Learned to live life in dissociative state,
to do what I should, which was wait on my mate.
I stayed in that marriage for 22 years.
'I deserve the abuse', I thought, through my tears.
But somehow I knew that the mindless control
strips us of spirit, robs us of soul.
I didn't know then that the childhood pain
sets us up for abuse again and again...

Years of therapy at exorbitant cost
trying to regain the self that was lost.
There are those that maintain it doesn't exist,
and that, my friends, is another knife twist.
One tries through exhaustion to climb out of the hole,
to regain the self that abusers have stole.
Years of rough work and weary of heart.
Years of wondering, just where do I start?
Years of uncertainty. Who am I now?
Memories surfacing, furrowing brow.
Too many shattered pieces of pain.
How can I put me together again?
Then, slowly, by trying, I found pieces of me.
Bit by bit new knowledge helped me to see.
I learned to find things that fill up my spirit,
and have now found a voice. I know others can hear it.
Each one, male and female, deserves to be heard.
We need listen with reverence when they speak a word.
For who of us knows the trials they've seen?
Who knows of the hellish places they've been?
'tis sharing together, the crimes of our past
that allows us to finally move forward at last.
Because my parents did nothing although they knew,
showed me my place. Into victim I grew.
Of course I forgive them. They just didn't know
the damage and turmoil into which I would grow.
It taught me my value, my place in the world...
that man takes whatever he wants from a girl.

The damage far-reaching, takes years to undo.
They would have protected me if only they knew.
Subscribed to belief, children seen and not heard
prevented them from listening to little girl's word.
Things were not talked about, oh no, they weren't then.
And so we kept silent again and again.
In spite of all this my eyes can now see
if I'd not walked where I've walked, I wouldn't be me.

CHOOSE

Be sure to live the life you choose.
When you don't, you lose, you lose.
What do you lose? What does it matter?
When you live life by rote? When your energies scatter?
One day you will likely awake
and think to yourself, "For My Goodness Sake."
You may well find yourself haunted
that you didn't do the things you wanted.
Instead you did what you thought you should
and missed out on so much. And that isn't good.
But wait!! It is now not too late
to spend valued time with your chosen mate.
Spend some time, too, with anyone else
who makes you feel good about self.
You will know this is true when you figure it out.
"This is what living is all about."

WHIP

Alright! That's it!! I'm hanging up my whip!
How much more blood do I need to feel drip?
How much more time spend in total despair?
How much more of this pain can I bear?

I can't live in that world and can't live in this.
Feel that my life is just one big abyss.
It seems all I know now is tears and more tears
I thought I'd already cried out through the years.

I'm lost in a place where I don't want to be.
I can't seem to find any comfort for me.
I've been trying and trying to make my life better
while the chains of the past continue to fetter.

I just do not know how to let myself be.
Every pain I have born is raining on me.
My biggest fear is that I've gone crazy
as the desire to live becomes murky and hazy.

Up, up, and again comes the feeling of shame.
At least now the feeling I feel has a name.
Years of work lets me know that the feeling is core
and I can't stand to feel it... No! Not anymore.

It ripples and cripples the person I am.
I want out of this life. I just don't give a damn.
I need to get out. I need it to cease.
Stop the pain. Stop the God awful pain please...

Out of Darkness Into Light

THE FAMILY WAITING

Life goes on, as we regroup and our whole focus scatters.
In order to stay sane, we know your murder matters.
We need to turn attention to picking up **our** pieces,
be present for the young - sons, daughters, nephews, nieces.
We need to start our lives anew, let go of the past.
It consumed us to our very souls. We let you go at last.
Doesn't mean we forget. You know we never will.
You live on in hearts and minds. The memories haunt us still.
Because we lost you physically, we've cried, been full of rage,
immersed ourselves in justice until we were **in** the cage.
It kept us moving forward with only you in mind
and we lost all sense of self, as if we were half blind.
Our other world ceased to exist, we gave up very life.
We forgot that we were daughter, sister, mother, wife.
And no matter what, we know our lives
will never be the same.
To do you justice, we must live. Ourselves we must reclaim!

BLAME

How many of us want to blame others
for all of our sorrows and stress?
We cannot conceive that we are the ones
who create our very own mess.
It is when we get that awareness
and our part becomes understood,
we can take charge of decisions.
Then we can make change for the good.
No longer playing the victim.
No longer placing the blame.
And this holds true, for me and for you.
Our lives are never the same!

LEAF

The little leaf flew all around
before it landed on the ground.
First it zigged and then it zagged.
Finally on some grass it snagged.
I watched it flying through the air
wafting softly, with a flair.
Amazing feelings flooded through
watching what this leaf could do.
That leaf's a lot like me and you
when we think with different view.
We zig. We zag, before we find
that sometimes we have been blind
to what's important in our life
and we stay mired in grief and strife.
Alas! There is some marvellous news.
We can change this if we choose
and land ourselves on firmer ground
instead of bouncing all around!

HEY MOM!

"Mom, hey Mom, it's snowing," he called out
in excitement as he tripped down the hallway.

Then he remembered.
She was not there.

He stopped.

In another house, she looks out the window
and knows he would want to share
his excitement with her.
And her face caves in.

She knows she needed to leave to survive,
but that does not stop her tears.

SUICIDE

What can we do for those so full of sorrow
it's impossible to envision a brighter tomorrow?
When the pain is so deep they can't find relief.
There is simply no way to cut through the grief.
All hope is gone, they feel only despair.
Although it's not true, they feel nobody cares.
No light in their lives. They feel only black.
And try as they will, cannot find their way back.
Energy gone, they're so tired of trying.
The only solution, they believe, is their dying...
Why don't we tell them we don't want 'them' to end?
Can we be there with them when they need a friend?
What are we willing to give, do, and be?
Is there an answer for them? Can I simply be me?
Can I open my eyes, and my mind and my heart?
Will I walk by their side? Yes! That is a start!
And maybe by being there as a friend
they will see life as beginning not end.

WHAT A RIDE

We've been there girl. We've done it all.
We've been beaten up and bruised.
We found our way right through the maize,
no longer feel so used.

Got through self-hate and depression.
We've finally hit our stride.
It's true. There's been some ups and downs
But holy smokes! What a ride!

LIFE

Life can be a challenge. Life can be so good.
Like does not always turn out the way we think it should.
We can do with it what we will, take it all in stride
or we can go away somewhere. Yes! We can run and hide.
How would we know the good times
if we never had some pain?
How could we know the sunshine if we never felt the rain?
What good would life be to us if everything was sun?
How could we deal with challenges if all we did was run?
We could not differentiate if each day was the same,
if we took no responsibility and all we did was blame.
Although sometimes it seems that way, life is not a race.
We will finish soon enough. Our ending we will face.
We miss the trip when we long for only destination
and forget to look with reverence at each and every station.
So let us all remember, the journey to enjoy
and as we traverse each day, our senses to employ.
Hear the birds, see the trees and stop to smell the flowers.
No matter what we do, or don't, they disappear, the hours.
So best we live our lives in full so we do not regret
and think that when we cannot 'do', we're not finished yet.
Now I sorely entreat you – do you get the gist?
Forget the things that are there on your 'To-Do' list.
Spend time with your loved ones. Spend it with a pet.
Therein lies good feelings. Sometimes we forget.
Think about the day-to-day ways that we are living.
Remember soul-filling joy we feel when we are giving.
Some of us fill our time, each day, by being busy.
We run around like crazy. My God, it makes me dizzy.

What is it we accomplish when we spread ourselves so thin?
Do we get to a place we have to be to find that we have been?
What is it we are doing? And how do we get whole?
What are the things that we can do to satisfy our soul?
Can we give to others? Lend a helping hand?
When someone needs comfort, can we understand?
Instead of feeling burdened and having need to judge,
so entrenched in our beliefs that we cannot budge.
We learned to act in certain ways. Oh Yes! We have. But wait!
Perhaps we can change who we've become,
and learn to tolerate.
I know that I can do it. Be who I want to be.
Because, you see, the choices, are always up to me!

NOT MY BUSINESS

Sometimes I get it. I confess,
judging others causes stress.
In going there, I do get caught
and know, my business, it is **not!**
Why think thoughts that cause me worry?
Am I police, and judge and jury?
'Cuz worrying what others do
is **not** my business. I know it's true!
And worrying what others think
can put me on the very brink
of craziness – as I obsess.
Good God! It ends in such a mess!
And who am I to judge at all?
when judging makes me feel quite small...
For it is just as I have thought
and know. My business, it is **not!**
Alas! My mind, it can be trained
to loosen fetters that have chained.
I believe we are the total sum
of our past, and where we're from.
But listen up. It might sound strange
but true. We have the power to change
who we are and what we think
by working hard to find the link
that path to be a better 'we'
and from all worrying be free.

It does not happen overnight
but it **will** happen when we fight
to find the ways where we feel good
with peace inside. Oh yes! We could.
For judging others is judging me
and that's **not** how I wish to be.

FACETS PROGRAM

When women come together with a common goal,
something very special happens to each and every soul.
There is no way that we can know at the very start
just how each and every woman will affect our heart.

As the weeks went flying by, I have come to know
that we all choose to be here, so we can learn and grow.
I think about our sessions, and upon each such reflection,
I not only **think**, but also **feel,** developing connection.

We learn to be yet more aware of each and every choice.
We learn as we go forward how to exercise our voice.
And as I learn, I make change. It gives my heart a lift.
Thanks Ursula, for the program, and each gal, for the gift!

HATRED

I sit here in fear,
crying yet.
Half numb,
on hold for the police.

It is frightening
to have someone
hate me so much
he wants to kill me.

The police tell me
they cannot
take my complaint.

I insist. It needs to be on record.

I have known
since I left
it is possible
he will kill me.

I need to know
that someone knows.

GAMES

And so, my dears, I refuse to play
the games you play.
I will not take part today.
You see, I've found a better way.
It brings me peace from day to day.
It helps me through – come what may.
And so,
I will not play the games you play.

RAGE

Where does your rage go when it's put to bed?
Does it go to sleep?
Does it dance in your head?
Of course, we all know that it would be best
to put all the rage that we feel to its rest.

What do we do with anger so deep
that it can cut like a knife?
We don't need to keep
it alive by stoking it day after day.
When we do, it is not only us who must pay.

The price of the anger that we keep within
and try to ignore, but cannot. We don't win
any peace for ourselves, serenity gone,
while we more often than not find ourselves all alone.

So what can we do when we find life's not fair?
We can stand up and face it, that is, if we dare
call a spade a spade. Walk away from the shit
and get on with our life. That's right. Go for it!!!

THE VAGINA MONOLOGUES

We *all* had a reason... we *all* had a cause,
a much larger reason than simple applause.
The reason is near and most dear to our heart.
In spite of our nerves, we wanted a part
in a play oh-so-great that it changes so much,
our thoughts, our wording, our actions and such.
The gift to our growing cannot be measured,
and for me, like the rest, will always be treasured.
Some didn't know the depth of the play
and as theory sunk in, felt some dismay
for these changes to thinking, the way we had been.
Could we make the adjustment? Remained to be seen.
Perhaps mostly for those of the 'old' generation
it created within agitated sensation.
And hey! We're in now. We're surely committed
and with each rehearsal, the power transmitted.
The strength engendered with reading each line
in spite of misgivings we knew we'd be fine.
Words hence unused came easy to lips
the way cake and ice cream stick to the hips.
There happened a bonding that was quick and was deep,
a feeling of camaraderie we know we can keep.
Supporting, and caring was rife in the room
growing in love like fetus in womb.
And I am so joyous for such education
and being part of this lasting sensation.
And! Oh my God... to be part of the cast
created a selection of memories to last.

EVIL

My eyes well up. My chest gets tight.
I will not give up without a fight.
I know they think that they have won
but they don't know it's just begun.

For I remember what they've done,
and Jesus Christ, they'd better run.
I'll live my memories and I'll get well
and they, those bastards, will rot in hell.

They prey on young who have no choice
but, as we grow, we find our voice.
Our numbers grow and we will tell
what they have done and we'll get well.

We'll band together and we are strong.
We had to be to get along.
And we will fight and we will win
and no longer will they pin

it all on us and hurt us so.
We will win. We'll make them go.
They played it out as if a game
while we will never be the same.

No more secrets, no more lies.
We see right through their big disguise.
And they're not strong. They're really weak.
Look close. You'll see their yellow streak.

They hide behind their secret wall.
Now we can see and we can call
them on their lies and their abuse
and let them know there is no use

for folks like them who only prey
on little ones. We've found our way.
Society will make them pay.
And we, the hurt, heal more each day.

LONELY

I thought I'd die of loneliness
left upon the shelf.
Since there was no else to love...
I learned to love myself.
I thought I'd die of loneliness,
married. Still alone.
No cure for all my ailments,
experience has shown.
I thought I'd die of loneliness
as I struggled to be free.
Can't stay close, nor yet apart.
I need serenity for me.

FRIENDS

We carry friends within our heart
when together, or apart.
Women have a way of sharing
burdens, successes, and lives, with caring.

There are many here who share the gift
of love, support. It gives a lift.
Sustains us when we're feeling down.
Helps us measure how we've grown.

Remember you are not alone,
when sometimes troubles feel full blown.
I carry you within my heart,
When we're together, or apart.

MY FRIEND

Simple words cannot express
the gratitude I feel
for the gift that you have given me,
a friendship warm and real.
Transcending time and distance
and holding ever true
sustaining me in sad times...
this is the gift of **_you_**.
I wish that we lived closer
and could have a cup of tea
as often as we want to.
That would be nice for me.
Here's hoping that your birthday
is as good as good can be.
Happy, Happy Birthday, Pat
wished to you... from me.

SUPPORT

Do you really know what happens when you
call someone a name?
You rob their soul and spirit. They cannot be the same.
What does it accomplish when you try to make them small?
Do you feel a better person? Does it make you ten feel tall?
Why get locked in arguments? Let others have their say.
It's okay if they are different. There'll be a brand new day.
They are the ones that need to choose what they think and do
don't put them down or criticize.
Don't make them choose like you.
Ah yes, it is a troubled world that we are living in,
but lift them up! Support them! and both of you will win!

INSIGHT

As I live my life, I read
inspiring thoughts. They plant a seed.
Oftentimes I need to write
providing insights so that I might
become who I was meant to be,
the loving person who is me.

For there is only love and fear.
The voices in my head I hear
would keep me trapped, must make them go,
replaced with loving thoughts. I know
I am the one who has the role
of choosing to expand my soul
with friends... I need those who seek.
Together we can get a peek
of ways of being that spirits lift.
As we transform, we see the gift.
Advancing soul... I feel connection
easing path with more reflection.
For if I stay so unaware
how can I change the things I dare?

The things I say, the things I do
from place of love. I want them true.
and as I *know*... feel this is how
must stay present, in the now.
And ahhhh... 'tis better, the way I feel.
My life today is much more real.
Far more soul-like. For this I strive.
And damn! It's good to be alive!

TIME

How precious is our time together.
Sometimes we forget
that time is very fleeting
and so we often let
the concerns of day to day
fill up to full, our mind.
When we find time to use our time
what is it that we find?

We find that there is no more,
that every second's used.
Indeed that we have squandered time
and we can feel quite bruised.
What happened to our time, we ask.
We feel it isn't fair
that when we finally reached for time
we find it isn't there.

So best we let our loved ones know
that we will take the time
to spend with them more often
Ah... that will be sublime.

TALKING

When I am talking and cannot be heard
I get to the place where I say not a word.
When others believe they have the right
to talk over me, it becomes quite a plight.
Do I continue the friendship? Or do I let go?
I'm sure there's an answer and I'd like to know.
It happens many times over and over again.
I swear to my God, it drives me insane.
I will not fight for a space in a group.
And what's more, right now, I don't give a poop.
I find it quite rude, and even uncouth.
I tell you right now, that's the God awful truth
I know there are folks who don't talk over so much,
who let one use their voice, who listen and such.
Now I need to decide if I want to walk
with gals who can't seem to allow me to talk.

GOTTA LEAVE

Oh Dear God, Dear God, I pray.
Please just let me get through today.
Let me bear the pain and sorrow,
knowing there will be a brighter tomorrow.
Help me find the strength I need
to not fold up. Oh this I plead.
I must get through. I must be strong
but all the while it feels so wrong.

When deep inside I feel so small
and all I want to do is howl.
The pieces of my soul are split
and everything has turned to shit.
I need the strength to get away —
cannot stay another day
pretending I can live this life
of drinking, loneliness, and strife.

While I put on a happy face
pretending it's an okay place,
I want to scream. I want to yell.
I know that I must leave this hell.
Don't know why it's hard to leave.
Another failure? More things to grieve?
I'm not afraid to be alone.
It feels like peace. It feels like home.
Where I can walk around my house,
not hide away like frightened mouse

from the man, his constant drink.
I need **away**. I need to **think**.
I know that living well brings peace.
Anxiety within will cease.
If I could go without a fight
I'd be away, right now. Tonight.

I'd leave and I would not look back
to life where there exists such lack.
He's willing to do anything, I think
as long as I don't mention drink.
As long as he can have his booze
this is the life he wants to choose.
I cannot stand another day,
must plan a simple getaway.

Don't want to live here anymore.
Don't know what I'm waiting for.
Magical thinking needs to go.
I need to think clear. I know
the answers always lie with me
so calm and peaceful I can be,
and live a life where I have choice,
where I feel peace and use my voice.
All right, Lin. It rests with you.
What the hell are you going to do?

FREE

Out of my need to be free comes the pain of regret
for all that we planned, the goals we had set.
Sometimes I wish that I could still be
the innocent person that once was me.

I strove to be all I could be for you,
thought I could be what you want me to.
Ever so slowly my awakening came.
When change is right, things can't stay the same.
No longer content to be one to serve,
I want so much more. I believe I deserve
to live in the way that only I can
and not simply be used by a man.

CHOICES

I can see that for my sake
it is imperative that I make
different choices than before,
because now, you see, I have more
information in my head,
no longer face a challenge with dread.
And quickly now, I can discern
they are the things by which I learn.
I also see I must expect
to be treated with respect.
Respect is what I choose to give.
It is the way I want to live.
We get in life what we allow.
And I allow much better now.
For it is by careful selecting
I get in life what I am expecting.
I understand the die is cast.
We are the sum total of our past.
Do not despair. Please! Take heart.
See each day as brand new start.
Dear, dear universe, this I ask,
help me to remove my mask.
Help me always strive to be
and share the very best of me.

BEAUTY

No, my dear, you need not stare.
I simply ask you be aware
of the beauty all around
and let serenity resound.

There's always beauty in the making
and it is there for all, for taking.
We can enjoy, or we cannot
depends which reality we've bought.

Are we aware? Are we tuned out?
We can choose, without a doubt.
To do so, we must really care.
Engage our senses. Be aware.
Big question is – DO WE DARE?

Fear of failure scares us silly.
We therefore rush so willy nilly.
Must do this and must do that.
Really? Is there where life's at?

Or can we stop and smell the flowers?
Can we take those countless hours?
Don't need "to do" but simply "be"
Oh! That is what I want for me.

HELP

Filled with anxiety,
judged by society,
I question my piety.
What will I decide?

Tense and full of fear,
afraid I'll disappear.
Can't keep my presence near.
Cannot run and hide.

Unbearable memories.
Oh please stop them, please.
Beggin' on my knees.
I cannot stand the ride.

Let me keep my sanity.
Let me have serenity.
Connect me with humanity.
Too many tears I've cried.

ABUSE

Do you know that abuse silently chips
the person we are? Oh yes! And it strips
us of our self-esteem.
Those who have been there know what I mean.
I've been writing poetry since eighty-nine,
although didn't know there'd come a time
for it all to go into a book
so others who falter may have a look
and know that they are not alone
when being abused cuts to the bone.

It may be that poems can help many others,
may comfort my sisters and comfort my brothers.
I've found a way to speak to those who feel lost.
They've already paid exorbitant cost.

I need to tell them. I need to shout —
with help, they, too, can lose all doubt
about who they are and what they're worth.
They have great value here on earth.
"Please hang on. You'll find your way
and live to sing another day."

I've been there. They'll hear my pain
and then will see I've found me again.
Before abuse I knew I was good
and now enjoy life like we all should.

CHANGE

Think of the women who don't want to live,
who fight a daily battle not to end their life.

Because they were abused,
stripped of their self-worth,
their identity.

Think of the women for whom it is too late,
who have no choice,
who are dying of cancer,
an end-product of abuse,
or who die at the hands of their abusers.

Think of these women and grieve.
Then, let that grief and compassion propel you.
Become aware of abuse and the need for change.
Remember the women and honour them
with a word, a gesture.
Begin to use your voice.

Remember, when one voice is joined by another,
and yet another, it is heard.

We must change. Change the way we are treated.

But first...

We need to change the way we see ourselves.

CHOOSE YOU

Because he cannot, will not, does not wish to see,
he uses our son to punish me.
Because I will no longer be his wife,
he wants to destroy the rest of my life.
To steal a heart, to use, control,
he takes from us our very soul.
We must always be and do
whatever he would want us to.

My son, my son, I grieve for you
and what you feel compelled to do.
He is the Dad you love and trust.
Obey the rules. You know you must
hate me, avoid me as you are told.
Run away. Do not let me hold
and hug you as I wish to do
because you are taught you can't be you.

Yes, my son, I grieve for you
and for my lost life I grieve for, too
as I was once inside your shoes
and finally knew I had to choose
to live his life, or live my own.
I decided. The seeds are sown.
For you, the choice is to stay
there with him. I hope and pray
that you won't wake up in pain one day
and know your life was taken away.

You have a right to think your thoughts.
You have a right to not feel caught
between us, your Mom and Dad...
who is good and who is bad.
This very right you are denied
and tears of sadness must be cried.
You have a right to the help you seek.
Oh don't give up and don't be meek.
Fight for you. You are good.
And you can talk, be understood.

Make your own choices.
You should be encouraged,
and not told you can't, and not be discouraged.
Live your own life. Find your own truth
and try to enjoy each day of your youth.

FREEING ME

I'll have my tears. I'll cry my cries,
and when I'm done, I'll dry my eyes.
Oh yes, I know that I could do
what other people what me to.

Pretend that everything's okay
and that it is a perfect day.
No problems here. We've mastered all.
Why then do I want to bawl?

My needs are met. There is no pain
of past inside, I say again.
I hide the pain behind this wall
even though it makes me small.

I'll have my tears. I'll cry my cries
and when I'm done, I'll dry my eyes.
For when I do, I then feel free
from pain inside that poisons me.

SMILE

When I'm down and see a smile
the lifted spirits stay awhile.
And we all know that smiles are free,
a delightful gift from you to me.
We also know that it is true
a smile's a gift from me to you.
We cannot know a stranger's sorrow
and how they might just dread tomorrow.
But since we have this gift to give
we must pass it on so others live
a moment with their burdens lifted
when another's smile to them is gifted.
And why not give? And why not share?
And why not show the world we care?

ABOUT THE AUTHOR

Lin Brian has been writing poetry for close to 30 years. Her poems have been published in newsletters, brochures, and programs, such as the Facets Program, based in her hometown of Oliver, British Columbia, Canada, Joseph Seiler's book, "Out of Paralysis," a true story, as well as the Gottman Institute in Seattle, Washington. She has been published in the Okanagan Tapestry, an anthology of Pentiction, British Columbia Writers. Lin has been contracted to write specific poems about specific people. This is her first book of poetry. It will be followed by two more, with poems selected from her collection. Several poems will be developed into children's books.

Made in the USA
San Bernardino, CA
20 March 2017